REFLECTIONS
FOR
LENT 2021

REFLECTIONS
FOR
LENT

17 February – 3 April 2021

MARK OAKLEY
MARGARET WHIPP
GRAHAM JAMES
GULI FRANCIS-DEHQANI

with an introduction by
MARK OAKLEY

Church House Publishing
Church House
Great Smith Street
London SW1P 3AZ

ISBN 978 1 78140 182 8

Published 2020 by Church House Publishing
Copyright © The Archbishops' Council 2020

The opinions expressed in this book are those of the
authors and do not necessarily reflect the official policy of
the General Synod or The Archbishops' Council of the
Church of England.

Liturgical editor: Peter Moger
Series editor: Hugh Hillyard-Parker
Designed and typeset by Hugh Hillyard-Parker
Copyedited by Ros Connelly
Printed by CPI Group (UK) Ltd, Croydon, CR0 4YY

What do you think of *Reflections for Lent*?

We'd love to hear from you – simply email us at

publishing@churchofengland.org

or write to us at

Church House Publishing, Church House,
Great Smith Street, London SW1P 3AZ.

Visit **www.dailyprayer.org.uk** for more
information on the *Reflections* series, ordering
and subscriptions.

Contents

About the authors

Stephen Cottrell is the Archbishop of York, having previously been Bishop of Chelmsford. He is a well-known writer and speaker on evangelism, spirituality and catechesis. He is one of the team that produced *Pilgrim*, the popular course for the Christian Journey.

Guli Francis-Dehqani was born in Iran but moved to England following the events of the 1979 Islamic Revolution. Having studied music as an undergraduate, she worked at the BBC for a few years before training for ordination and completing a PhD. She was ordained in 1998 and has served as Bishop of Loughborough since 2017.

Graham James was Bishop of Norwich for almost 20 years until his retirement in 2019. Since then he has chaired the Paterson Inquiry, an independent inquiry for the Government on patient safety in the NHS and private healthcare. Earlier in his ministry he was Bishop of St Germans in his native Cornwall and Chaplain to two Archbishops of Canterbury. His most recent book is *A Place for God* about the relationship between location and faith.

Mark Oakley is Dean and Fellow of St John's College, Cambridge, and Honorary Canon Theologian of Wakefield Cathedral in the Diocese of Leeds. He is the author of *The Collage of God* (2001), *The Splash of Words: Believing in Poetry* (2016), and *My Sour Sweet Days: George Herbert and the Journey of the Soul* (2019) as well as articles and reviews, usually in the areas of faith, poetry, human rights and literature. He is Visiting Lecturer in the department of Theology and Religious Studies at King's College London.

Rachel Treweek is Bishop of Gloucester and the first female diocesan bishop in England. She served in two parishes in London and was Archdeacon of Northolt and later Hackney. Prior to ordination she was a speech and language therapist and is a trained practitioner in conflict transformation.

Margaret Whipp is an Anglican priest and spiritual director based in Oxford. Her first career was in medicine. Since ordination in 1990, she has ministered in parish and chaplaincies and served in theological education. Her books include the *SCM Studyguide in Pastoral Theology* and *The Grace of Waiting*.

About *Reflections for Lent*

Based on the *Common Worship Lectionary* readings for Morning Prayer, these daily reflections are designed to refresh and inspire times of personal prayer. The aim is to provide rich, contemporary and engaging insights into Scripture.

Each page lists the lectionary readings for the day, with the main psalms for that day highlighted in **bold**. The collect of the day – either the *Common Worship* collect or the shorter additional collect – is also included.

For those using this book in conjunction with a service of Morning Prayer, the following conventions apply: a psalm printed in parentheses is omitted if it has been used as the opening canticle at that office; a psalm marked with an asterisk may be shortened if desired.

A short reflection is provided on either the Old or New Testament reading. Popular writers, experienced ministers, biblical scholars and theologians contribute to this series, all bringing their own emphases, enthusiasms and approaches to biblical interpretation.

Regular users of Morning Prayer and *Time to Pray* (from *Common Worship: Daily Prayer*) and anyone who follows the Lectionary for their regular Bible reading will benefit from the rich variety of traditions represented in these stimulating and accessible pieces.

The book also includes both a simple form of Common Worship: Morning Prayer (see pages 48–49) and a short form of Night Prayer, also known as Compline (see pages 52–55), particularly for the benefit of those readers who are new to the habit of the Daily Office or for any reader while travelling.

Lent – jousting within the self

It has been said that the heart of the human problem is the problem of the human heart. Lent is time set aside each year to take this thought seriously.

A few years ago, there was a story in the papers about a painting by Pieter Bruegel the Elder. It is currently on display in Vienna's marvellous Kunsthistorisches Museum, but Krakow's National Museum claims it is theirs and that it was stolen by the wife of the city's Nazi governor in 1939 during the occupation of Poland.

The painting is called 'The Fight Between Carnival and Lent' and it was painted in 1559. It is a beautifully typical Bruegel painting. It is a large, crowded canvas with nearly 200 men, women and children depicted on it. We find ourselves looking down on a town square during a riotous festival. The painting can be looked at in two halves. On the right, we see a church with people leaving after prayer. We see them giving alms to the poor, feeding the hungry, helping those with disability, calling attention to their need and tending to the dying. On the left, we see an inn. Congregated around it are beer drinkers, gamblers, various saucy types. The vulnerable nearby are not noticed, including a solitary procession of lepers. Instead, a man vomits out of a window and another bangs his head against a wall.

In the foreground, we see two figures being pulled towards each other on floats. One is Lady Lent, gaunt and unshowy, dressed as a nun, with followers eating pretzels and fish as well as drawing fresh water from a large well. The other is Carnival, a fat figure, armed with a meat spit and a pork pie helmet. He's followed by masked carousers. A man in yellow – the symbolic colour of deceit – pushes his float, though he looks rather weighed down by cups and a bag of belongings. In the background, we see, on the left, some stark, leafless trees, but on the right side, buds are awakening on the branches and, as if to see them better, a woman is busily cleaning her windows.

It is an allegorical delight, and we might do worse than take a close look at it sometime this Lent. It's tempting to classify each human there as either good or bad, secular or faithful, kind or indifferent. We love to place people into convenient cutlery trays, dividing us all up as is most useful for us. What I love about this painting, however, is that it reminds me that we are all similarly made with two halves.

For so many of us, there is a constant fight going on within between the times we are negligent and the times we are careful; days in which we get through with a self that enjoys its own attention, being centre-stage, and days when our self just feels somehow more itself when not being selfish. I have an impulse to pray; I have an impulse to avoid or forget it. There are parts of me grotesquely masked, and there are parts of me trying to clean my windows on a ladder, as it were, wanting to increase transparency and attention to the world, to me and to my relationships.

Lent begins with a small dusty cross being made on my head, the hard case that protects the organ that makes decisions. The season starts by asking me to imagine how life might be if the imprint of Christ's courageous compassion might make itself felt and acted on, rather than just passionately talked about. Lent knows what we are like. It has seen the painting. It has read a bit of Freud, some history books, political manifestos and memoirs of hurt and achievement. It winces at our cyclical, self-destructive repetitions. It believes in us, though, knowing that, with God and each other, if we reach outside of our own hardened little worlds, we set the scene to be helped and, maybe, even changed. That would be good – for me and those who live with me.

In the Gospels, the 40 days Jesus spent in the beguiling wilderness immediately followed his baptism. Coming up out of the water, he had heard the unmistakable voice that matters, telling him he was cherished, wanted and ready. He then goes into the heat spending time with himself, hearing other voices that want him to live down to them; but he knows that his vocation can only be lived when he learns to live up to the one voice he heard that day in the river, not down to the ones that want him to live some conventionally indifferent and submerged existence as a consumer of the world and not as a citizen of the kingdom. We follow him. Where he goes, so do we. A wilderness Lent is needed more than ever to do some heart-repair and start becoming Christians again.

I don't know who owns the Bruegel painting. What I do know is that its themes belong to all of us; our inner landscape matches his rowdy town square. As long as the fight continues, the soul will be alive.

Mark Oakley

3

Building daily prayer into daily life

In our morning routines there are many tasks we do without giving much thought to them, and others that we do with careful attention. Daily prayer and Bible reading is a strange mixture of these. These are disciplines (and gifts) that we as Christians should have in our daily pattern, but they are not tasks to be ticked off. Rather they are a key component of our developing relationship with God. In them is *life* – for the fruits of this time are to be lived out by us – and to be most fruitful, the task requires both purpose and letting go.

In saying a daily office of prayer, we make a deliberate decision to spend time with God – the God who is always with us. In prayer and attentive reading of the Scriptures, there is both a conscious entering into God's presence and a 'letting go' of all we strive to control: both are our acknowledgement that it is God who is God.

> *... come before his presence with a song...*
>
> *Know that the Lord is God;*
> *it is he that has made us and we are his;*
> *we are his people and the sheep of his pasture.*
>
> *Enter his gates with thanksgiving...*
>
> *(Psalm 100, a traditional Canticle at Morning Prayer)*

If we want a relationship with someone to deepen and grow, we need to spend time with that person. It can be no surprise that the same is true between us and God.

In our daily routines, I suspect that most of us intentionally look in the mirror; occasionally we might see beyond the surface of our external reflection and catch a glimpse of who we truly are. For me, a regular pattern of daily prayer and Bible reading is like a hard look in a clean mirror: it gives a clear reflection of myself, my life and the world in which I live. But it is more than that, for in it I can also see the reflection of God who is most clearly revealed in Jesus Christ and present with us now in the Holy Spirit.

This commitment to daily prayer is about our relationship with the God who is love. St Paul, in his great passage about love, speaks of now seeing 'in a mirror, dimly' but one day seeing face to face: 'Now I know only in part; then I will know fully, even as I have been fully known' (1 Corinthians 13.12). Our daily prayer is part of that seeing in a mirror dimly, and it is also part of our deep yearning for an ever-clearer vision of our God. As we read Scripture, the past and the future converge in the present moment. We hear words from long ago – some of which can appear strange and confusing – and yet, the Holy Spirit is living and active in the present. In this place of relationship and revelation, we open ourselves to the possibility of being changed, of being reshaped in a way that is good for us and all creation.

It is important that the words of prayer and scripture should penetrate deep within rather than be a mere veneer. A quiet location is therefore a helpful starting point. For some, domestic circumstances or daily schedule make that difficult, but it is never impossible to become more fully present to God. The depths of our being can still be accessed no matter the world's clamour and activity. An awareness of this is all part of our journey from a false sense of control to a place of letting go, to a place where there is an opportunity for transformation.

Sometimes in our attention to Scripture there will be connection with places of joy or pain; we might be encouraged or provoked or both. As we look and see and encounter God more deeply, there will be thanksgiving and repentance; the cries of our heart will surface as we acknowledge our needs and desires for ourselves and the world. The liturgy of Morning Prayer gives this voice and space.

I find it helpful to begin Morning Prayer by lighting a candle. This marks my sense of purpose and my acknowledgement of Christ's presence with me. It is also a silent prayer for illumination as I prepare to be attentive to what I see in the mirror, both of myself and of God. Amid the revelation of Scripture and the cries of my heart, the constancy of the tiny flame bears witness to the hope and light of Christ in all that is and will be.

When the candle is extinguished, I try to be still as I watch the smoke disappear. For me, it is symbolic of my prayers merging with the day. I know that my prayer and the reading of Scripture are not the smoke and mirrors of delusion. Rather, they are about encounter and discovery as I seek to venture into the day to love and serve the Lord as a disciple of Jesus Christ.

+ Rachel Treweek

Lectio Divina – a way of reading the Bible

Lectio Divina is a contemplative way of reading the Bible. It dates back to the early centuries of the Christian Church and was established as a monastic practice by Benedict in the sixth century. It is a way of praying the Scriptures that leads us deeper into God's word. We slow down. We read a short passage more than once. We chew it over slowly and carefully. We savour it. Scripture begins to speak to us in a new way. It speaks to us personally, and aids that union we have with God through Christ, who is himself the Living Word.

Make sure you are sitting comfortably. Breathe slowly and deeply. Ask God to speak to you through the passage that you are about to read.

This way of praying starts with our silence. We often make the mistake of thinking prayer is about what we say to God. It is actually the other way round. God wants to speak to us. He will do this through the Scriptures. So don't worry about what to say. Don't worry if nothing jumps out at you at first. God is patient. He will wait for the opportunity to get in. He will give you a word and lead you to understand its meaning for you today.

First reading: Listen
As you read the passage listen for a word or phrase that attracts you. Allow it to arise from the passage as if it is God's word for you today. Sit in silence repeating the word or phrase in your head.

Then say the word or phrase aloud.

Second reading: Ponder
As you read the passage again, ask how this word or phrase speaks to your life and why it has connected with you. Ponder it carefully. Don't worry if you get distracted – it may be part of your response to offer to God. Sit in silence and then frame a single sentence that begins to say aloud what this word or phrase says to you.

Third reading: Pray

As you read the passage for the last time, ask what Christ is calling from you. What is it that you need to do or consider or relinquish or take on as a result of what God is saying to you in this word or phrase? In the silence that follows the reading, pray for the grace of the Spirit to plant this word in your heart.

If you are in a group, talk for a few minutes and pray with each other.

If you are on your own, speak your prayer to God either aloud or in the silence of your heart.

If there is time, you may even want to read the passage a fourth time, and then end with the same silence before God with which you began.

++Stephen Cottrell

Wednesday 17 February
Ash Wednesday

Psalm **38**
Daniel 9.3-6, 17-19
1 Timothy 6.6-19

1 Timothy 6.6-19

'... pursue righteousness, godliness, faith, love, endurance, gentleness' (v.11)

Lent is a snowfall in the soul. Just as snow makes us see our landscape in a different light, making us renavigate our environment and wonder at the sight of our own breath, so Lent invites us to distil, reimagine and remember the fragile miracle of our own self.

We are reminded here that we brought nothing into the world and will take nothing out. As ash is placed on our head today, the cross is placed on the heads that house our brains, the centres of our will power and decision-making. These are being called back to life, to a balanced sense and a proportionate understanding of ourselves. Along with Timothy, we are encouraged to pursue love, gentleness and what is right. This letter, like Lent, asks us to stop being indifferent, cautious and compromised. It speaks of the 'life that really is life', the one that is activated and sustained by love of God and our neighbour.

Time presses upon us and tells us we're too busy to be reflective, but our souls know better. Souls die from lack of reflection. Unawareness, like money, is a root of all evil too. Responsibilities distract us and tell us we're too involved with the 'real' world to be concerned about the spiritual questions. But it is always spiritual questions that make the difference in the way we go about our public and day-to-day lives.

COLLECT

Almighty and everlasting God,
you hate nothing that you have made
and forgive the sins of all those who are penitent:
create and make in us new and contrite hearts
that we, worthily lamenting our sins
and acknowledging our wretchedness,
may receive from you, the God of all mercy,
perfect remission and forgiveness;
through Jesus Christ your Son our Lord,
who is alive and reigns with you,
in the unity of the Holy Spirit,
one God, now and for ever.

Reflection by **Mark Oakley**

Psalm **77** *or* 56, **57** (63*)   **Thursday 18 February**
Jeremiah 2.14-32
John 4.1-26

John 4.1-26

*'God is spirit, and those who worship him must worship in spirit
and truth' (v.24)*

As a Jewish male, Jesus is in a position of advantage over this woman,
but as a thirsty traveller, he is obviously at a disadvantage. Jesus
invites the dialogue by becoming vulnerable ('Give me a drink') and
by allowing the woman to exercise some power over him. The scene
is paradoxical. Here is the giver of living water, thirsty himself.
A thirsty Messiah and a resourceful woman will find out that they
need each other. It is a beautiful metaphor for how God and
humanity are intimately interconnected.

Their conversation is one for a parched society. The Victorian poet
and priest Gerard Manley Hopkins prayed that our roots would be
sent rain, and similarly here we understand that the dryness of life
needs the water, the teaching and the Spirit of Christ if anything is
to grow in us.

Jesus says that God is spirit and that we must worship in truth. It is
said that the Church talks a lot about truth but finds honesty
difficult. Maybe being truthful is one sure way of worshipping God
and might be more acceptable to God than half-hearted pieties and
self-proclaiming certainties?

Holy God,
our lives are laid open before you:
rescue us from the chaos of sin
and through the death of your Son
bring us healing and make us whole
in Jesus Christ our Lord.

COLLECT

Reflection by **Mark Oakley**   9

Friday 19 February

John 4.27-42

'Come and see a man who told me everything I have ever done!'
(v.29)

St John's Gospel has an emphasis on Jesus as light, and we here find the Samaritan woman celebrating the fact with her friends that Jesus has told her everything that she's done in life. I'm not quite sure that's something I'd be very comfortable with! The woman, on the other hand, wants others to see how light thrown on you changes your life.

There is talk of judgement in the Christian faith and some reference to it in John's Gospel. We often have in mind the medieval pictures of torment as wicked souls are tossed into hell. In this encounter, though, we find a very different truth. Here judgement is liberating. The woman, at last, has confronted who she is and has done it with her new friend who took the time to value her and even seek her help. We often fear God not because God is angry but because God is real and we aren't. We are hidden in masks and disguises, deceitful even to ourselves. The judgement of the gospel is ultimately a relief as all this is taken off us and we stand before God as we are, in all our beauty and need.

The Samaritan woman's cause for evangelism is that she has nothing to hide any longer thanks to her encounter with Jesus at a well. What she is has been valued and loved, and now the living water will start, we don't doubt, to make her grow in spirit even more.

COLLECT

Almighty and everlasting God,
you hate nothing that you have made
and forgive the sins of all those who are penitent:
create and make in us new and contrite hearts
that we, worthily lamenting our sins
and acknowledging our wretchedness,
may receive from you, the God of all mercy,
perfect remission and forgiveness;
through Jesus Christ your Son our Lord,
who is alive and reigns with you,
in the unity of the Holy Spirit,
one God, now and for ever.

Reflection by **Mark Oakley**

Psalm **71** *or* **68**
Jeremiah 4.1-18
John 4.43-end

Saturday 20 February

John 4.43-end

'Unless you see signs and wonders you will not believe' (v.48)

Throughout his Gospel, John shares seven signs that Jesus performs, each revealing something significant about Jesus' identity and mission. Early in the story, Jesus turns water into wine – and not just wine, but the best wine in vast quantities – revealing the profound abundance of God in Jesus, what is earlier described as 'grace upon grace' (1.16). In this scene, Jesus heals the son of a royal official revealing his opposition to those things that keep abundant life from the children of God and his ability to restore health and life.

The official is a man used to giving orders, but here he comes begging for Jesus to save the life of his child. Jesus seems irritated that miracles and signs are needed before people believe, but the man doesn't seem to hear and just wants help. Such open love and honest raw need is the path that leads to healing. He doesn't enter doctrinal or language games with Jesus in order to get a miracle and have his faith confirmed.

The Gospel of John is a book of signs pointing to the recklessly loving grace of God. Like the Bible, life itself is to be read by us with attentiveness so we can read the love between the lines and find ourselves full of gratitude, which, when it comes, is not only a miracle in itself but allows us to see so many more.

Holy God,
our lives are laid open before you:
rescue us from the chaos of sin
and through the death of your Son
bring us healing and make us whole
in Jesus Christ our Lord.

COLLECT

Reflection by **Mark Oakley**   11

Monday 22 February

Psalms 10, 11 *or* 71
Jeremiah 4.19-end
John 5.1-18

John 5.1-18

'Do you want to be made well?' (v.6)

Jesus performs another mighty work. The scene shifts to a healing sanctuary in Jerusalem, where many unfortunates gather around the miraculous pool. Between them they represent every kind of malady – 'blind, lame, and paralysed'. As often in the Gospel stories, the reader is alert to deeper allusions. This group of invalids stands for all that is wanting in human vision, motivation and strength.

Among them, Jesus singles out one man lying on a pallet. He is scarcely a sympathetic character, perhaps one of those people who make your heart sink, who has lain in a piteous state for decades. Complaining that no one will help him, we sense that he is as passive spiritually as he is impotent physically. Jesus' invitation is direct and incisive: 'Do you want to be made well?'

Like a swirling kaleidoscope, the story reflects layers of symbolic meaning, unfolding a rich significance in Jesus' mighty works. This man has been weak and sickly for 38 years, the same length of time the Jews wandered helplessly in the wilderness, waiting for God's promise to be fulfilled (Deuteronomy 2.14).

We notice the detail that this healing takes place on a sabbath: the day when God's people and the whole creation are restored and renewed. Far from resting idle at such a time, Jesus speaks out to challenge the enervating faithlessness in both individuals and nations. 'Stand up, take your mat and walk!'

COLLECT | Almighty God,
whose Son Jesus Christ fasted forty days in the wilderness,
and was tempted as we are, yet without sin:
give us grace to discipline ourselves in obedience to your Spirit;
and, as you know our weakness,
so may we know your power to save;
through Jesus Christ your Son our Lord,
who is alive and reigns with you,
in the unity of the Holy Spirit,
one God, now and for ever.

12 | *Reflection by* **Margaret Whipp**

Psalm **44** *or* **73**
Jeremiah 5.1-19
John 5.19-29

Tuesday 23 February

John 5.19-29

'... whatever the Father does, the Son does likewise' (v.19)

After the mighty work comes a reaction. Jesus' audacious behaviour provokes fury among those who fear for the sanctity of the sabbath. Just who does this man think he is?

'Amen, Amen,' responds Jesus. The Greek phrase translated as 'very truly' introduces a solemn pronouncement, as Jesus speaks of the holy and intimate relationship with his Father God.

The evangelist's theology at this point is reverent and very carefully weighed. Far from the casual blasphemy alleged by his pious critics, Jesus' speech does not set himself up to subvert God's authority. His stance is, in fact, the very opposite of a rebellious child. All that Jesus seeks to be and to do sits in humble relationship with his Father; he seeks no autonomous status or will. This is his staggering claim of a kind of sonship, which is at once both radically empowering and profoundly submissive.

At the heart of this filial relationship is love. The God who 'so loved the world' (John 3.16) now entrusts his beloved Son with the knowledge of his purpose and the priceless gift of eternal life.

Jesus is determined to do 'only what he sees the Father doing'. When we reflect on our own place in God's loving mission here on earth, how much do we reflect the same faithfulness and intimate dependence?

COLLECT

Heavenly Father,
your Son battled with the powers of darkness,
and grew closer to you in the desert:
help us to use these days to grow in wisdom and prayer
that we may witness to your saving love
in Jesus Christ our Lord.

Wednesday 24 February

Psalms **6**, 17 *or* **77**
Jeremiah 5.20-end
John 5.30-end

John 5.30-end

'I do not accept glory from human beings' (v.41)

The polemical debate is ratcheting up. Jesus' enemies, in a foretaste of the trial to come, question the source of his bold authority. How can he make such claims for himself? Where is the evidence; and who are his witnesses?

Ironically, it is Jesus' accusers who are really on trial. They are the ones who protect their privilege through cosy structures of human approval, 'for they loved human glory more than the glory that comes from God' (John 12.43). Jesus has no time for 'old-boy' networks. His one concern is to be fully faithful to his divine calling. For those with eyes to see, it is self-evident that Jesus reflects his Father's glory – 'glory as of a father's only son, full of grace and truth' (John 1.14).

How tragic it is when religious leaders, picking zealously over scriptural niceties, entirely miss their main thrust. It is culpable blindness to reject the burning evidence of authority in Jesus' life, to which those scriptures, along with the Baptist's testimony, bear eloquent witness.

The very best of religion can be perverted by self-seeking power. When we seek glory from one another, in our mutual back-slapping and tribalism, our churches become closed and self-sufficient with no appetite for the true glory that comes from God. Could our own religious networks be corrupted through such smugness?

COLLECT

Almighty God,
whose Son Jesus Christ fasted forty days in the wilderness,
and was tempted as we are, yet without sin:
give us grace to discipline ourselves in obedience to your Spirit;
and, as you know our weakness,
so may we know your power to save;
through Jesus Christ your Son our Lord,
who is alive and reigns with you,
in the unity of the Holy Spirit,
one God, now and for ever.

Reflection by **Margaret Whipp**

Psalms **42**, 43 *or* **78.1-39***
Jeremiah 6.9-21
John 6.1-15

Thursday 25 February

John 6.1-15

'Now the Passover ... was near' (v.4)

We know this story very well. All four Gospels present an account of the miraculous feeding of a multitude. Typically, the fourth Gospel provides a distinctively theological reading of the event. It is one of the great 'signs' that will introduce a profound reflection on Jesus, the living Bread of Life.

Why mention the small detail of the approaching Passover festival? This incidental fact earths the timing of the miracle in the spring season, when the grass is abundant and green. But, more suggestively, it also points forward to the ultimate sign of Jesus' glory revealed in his Passover sacrifice for the sins of the world.

The story is wonderfully told, to be relished at every level. We can smile at the cluelessness of the disciples, and the ludicrously meagre resources snatched from the hands of a little lad. We are hushed as Jesus gives thanks over the bread – the Greek verb denotes our word for Eucharist. And we are heartened by the Lord's insistence that all the scattered fragments will be gloriously gathered up.

Week by week, believers across the world celebrate the Eucharist as a foretaste of the heavenly banquet prepared for all peoples. Still taking nothing grander than our small, perishable offerings, Christ satisfies our deepest hunger for eternal and imperishable food. People who first saw this sign began to appreciate its phenomenal significance. Do we?

Heavenly Father,
your Son battled with the powers of darkness,
and grew closer to you in the desert:
help us to use these days to grow in wisdom and prayer
that we may witness to your saving love
in Jesus Christ our Lord.

COLLECT

Friday 26 February

Psalm **22** *or* **55**
Jeremiah 6.22-end
John 6.16-27

John 6.16-27

'It is I; do not be afraid' (v.20)

Four words, in the vivid Greek narration of this drama, tell us everything we need to know about Jesus. 'I AM; FEAR NOT.' Into the midst of the storm, Jesus comes, bearing divine reassurance and peace.

Hebrew literature is full of dark stories about the raging of the sea. In graphic detail, Psalm 77 describes one of those elemental storms: 'the clouds poured out water, the skies thundered; your arrows flashed on every side' (Psalm 77.17). Meditating on God's power to redeem, the psalm recalls how the Lord strode through mighty waters, making a path through the heaving seas. The imagery is unforgettable and the meaning unambiguous: the one who walks through stormy seas is none other than the almighty Lord himself.

Did the disciples begin to grasp this? The story tells how, as they crossed the sea in their small boat, it grew dark, such that they could not see Jesus. Surprised by the ferocity of the storm, they became suddenly aware of the nearness of the Lord; yet, even then, they were terrified and hesitated to take him into the boat.

Buffeted by anxious times, all Christians know these archetypal fears. When we are overwhelmed by forces too strong for us, even in the pitch of night, Christ comes close – to reassure, to speak peace, to step right into our lives, to guide us to our safe haven.

'It is I; do not be afraid.'

COLLECT

Almighty God,
whose Son Jesus Christ fasted forty days in the wilderness,
and was tempted as we are, yet without sin:
give us grace to discipline ourselves in obedience to your Spirit;
and, as you know our weakness,
so may we know your power to save;
through Jesus Christ your Son our Lord,
who is alive and reigns with you,
in the unity of the Holy Spirit,
one God, now and for ever.

| *Reflection by* **Margaret Whipp**

Saturday 27 February

John 6.27-40

'I am the bread of life' (v.35)

Little by little, the glorious vision of the Fourth Gospel continues to unfold. Jesus first utters the majestic phrase, 'I am', at the calming of the tempest earlier in the chapter. Now we begin to glimpse the vast depth of meaning set forth in those words.

'I am' is nothing less than an emphatic expression of divine origin, and of personal union with God. Moses, trembling before the burning bush, was the first to receive the revelation of the Lord's name in mysterious terms. Translators, quite naturally, struggle to render the enormity of this designation, which concentrates all the energy of the verb 'to be'. How can human thought or language begin to apprehend the truth of a name that is given as 'I AM WHO I AM', or simply 'I AM'? (Exodus 3.14-15).

Here in the gospel of Jesus, we begin to see with our own eyes and grasp with our own hands the electrifying immanence of this divine aliveness. Step by step, the evangelist will take us deeper into this mystery, through seven momentous sayings on the lips of Jesus.

'I AM the bread of life.' Like manna in the wilderness, yet so much more, Jesus satisfies our aching hunger. His gift is as earthy as bread, and as heavenly as life eternal: it is the gift of his own self.

'Lord, give us this bread always!'

Heavenly Father,
your Son battled with the powers of darkness,
and grew closer to you in the desert:
help us to use these days to grow in wisdom and prayer
that we may witness to your saving love
in Jesus Christ our Lord.

COLLECT

Reflection by **Margaret Whipp** | 17

Monday I March

John 6.41-51

'Is not this ... the son of Joseph?' (v.42)

Here come the objections! Bold claims on the lips of Jesus provoke outrage and bewilderment in his hearers. He talks about coming down from heaven; but many of those listening know very well the earthly context of his family and upbringing. Their disdainful attitude shows how familiarity breeds contempt.

The evangelist notes their 'murmuring' (KJV). The word is reminiscent of the fault-finding attitude of the Israelites in the wilderness who were dissatisfied with God's generous provision for their physical needs (Exodus 16.2,7-12). Now something far greater than manna is set forth for God's people – if only they have eyes to see.

'I am the bread of life.' Jesus repeats the startling revelation. Unlike the lifeless manna of the desert, Jesus stands before them in all the fullness of life. And, unlike our mundane food that must perish and be replaced from day to day, the food that Jesus offers will endure for ever.

The whole mystery of the incarnation is contained in these words. Jesus is always lifting our gaze from the earthly plane to heavenly realities. For the cynic, it is laughable that this ordinary man from Nazareth should present himself as coming down from heaven. But for those whose hearts are open to the grace of God, this 'son of Joseph' is the very embodiment of life eternal – here, now, and dwelling among us.

COLLECT

Almighty God,
you show to those who are in error the light of your truth,
that they may return to the way of righteousness:
grant to all those who are admitted
    into the fellowship of Christ's religion,
that they may reject those things
    that are contrary to their profession,
and follow all such things as are agreeable to the same;
through our Lord Jesus Christ,
who is alive and reigns with you,
in the unity of the Holy Spirit,
one God, now and for ever.

Reflection by **Margaret Whipp**

Tuesday 2 March

John 6.52-59

'Those who eat my flesh and drink my blood' (v.56)

We have come a long way from the picnic on the hillside. Through rich layers of figurative language, the evangelist draws our attention ever deeper into the full meaning of Jesus' life and death. Today's reflection carries a profound message for contemporary Christians who, like the first gospel readers, still meet Jesus in the Eucharist.

'How can this man give us his flesh to eat?' It is a shocking image, one that forces us to face the connections between death and life, sacrifice and self-giving. The only way that Jesus' flesh can become life-giving food for others will be through his death. His blood, which in Jewish thinking was such a sacred life-force, will be released only through brutal sacrifice. These everyday metaphors of eating and drinking are radically disrupted and transcended.

The invitation to believers is to partake. We must eat and drink if we are to know eternal life. Jesus insists on this act of most intimate communion: it is through his own indwelling that we will share in the divine union itself.

Such daring theology invites argument and mocking disbelief. Then as now, there are many who find it all, quite literally, too much to swallow. Yet still Jesus calls to the table those who have much faith and those who can only seek a little more: to feed on him in our hearts with thanksgiving.

COLLECT

Almighty God,
by the prayer and discipline of Lent
may we enter into the mystery of Christ's sufferings,
and by following in his Way
come to share in his glory;
through Jesus Christ our Lord.

Reflection by **Margaret Whipp** | 19

Wednesday 3 March

Psalm **35** *or* **119.105-128**
Jeremiah 8.18 – 9.11
John 6.60-end

John 6.60-end

'Lord, to whom can we go?' (v.68)

We reach a watershed moment for the disciples. Following this Jesus is no longer easy, or consoling, or pretty. His stark language provokes a disturbing response, a sifting of commitment. Not for the first time, we encounter Jesus as a figure of division. Large crowds may be eager to follow him for as long as he remains a popular miracle-worker. But, when it is no longer convenient or fashionable, we read that many 'turned back and no longer went about with him'.

Jesus applies no coercion or emotional pressure to these lukewarm adherents: he simply lets them go. But to his inner Twelve, Jesus puts the haunting question: 'Do you also wish to go away?' He cuts straight to the heart. Times of ambivalence and confusion are unavoidable, but Jesus' challenge touches the core of motivation and will.

Simon Peter's agonized response is heartening to any later disciple who experiences their faith, at times, to be horribly uncertain, conflicted, or downright painful. 'To whom can we go?' These words, dredged from the depths of Peter's soul, tell how completely he has come to trust in this Jesus. He speaks for all of us who have found nowhere else such life-giving purpose and peace.

Times of crisis will test our faith to the marrow. For Peter, his wavering faith grew stronger, bearing witness as never before: 'you are the Holy One of God!'

COLLECT

Almighty God,
you show to those who are in error the light of your truth,
that they may return to the way of righteousness:
grant to all those who are admitted
    into the fellowship of Christ's religion,
that they may reject those things
    that are contrary to their profession,
and follow all such things as are agreeable to the same;
through our Lord Jesus Christ,
who is alive and reigns with you,
in the unity of the Holy Spirit,
one God, now and for ever.

Reflection by **Margaret Whipp**

Psalm **34** *or* 90, **92**
Jeremiah 9.12-24
John 7.1-13

Thursday 4 March

John 7.1-13

'My time has not yet come' (v.6)

Tension and danger now surround Jesus and his disciples. Their movements are being watched. Jesus is a subversive figure of close interest to the authorities, and we know it is no exaggeration that they are seeking an opportunity to kill him.

How will Jesus respond? Here, as in other parts of the Gospel, his family are keen to come forward with advice. A great festival is approaching when Jerusalem will be packed out with pilgrims. Why not play to the crowds, and take the limelight through a very public display of signs and miracles?

Jesus is unmoved by this fallacious strategy. He is not a populist leader seeking fame and following for his cause. He keeps his counsel, choosing instead to proceed to the festival in his own way and his own time.

Once again, we are astonished at the clear-sighted calm with which Jesus makes his decisions. He is not pushed back and forth, whether by fear or by fortune, but presses steadily forward to fulfil his divine vocation. His overriding concern is to be faithful to God's timing and purpose, even though his path to glory must bring a uniquely personal cost.

In a fearful world, where leaders and influencers jostle for the slightest tactical advantage, such poise and discernment are very rare qualities indeed.

Almighty God,
by the prayer and discipline of Lent
may we enter into the mystery of Christ's sufferings,
and by following in his Way
come to share in his glory;
through Jesus Christ our Lord.

COLLECT

Reflection by **Margaret Whipp** | 21

Friday 5 March

John 7.14-24

'Jesus went up into the temple and began to teach' (v.14)

If Jesus is trying to avoid a confrontation in Jerusalem, this is not the most sensible way to proceed. Perhaps influenced by the prophetic image (Malachi 3.1), the evangelist describes Jesus' sudden appearance in the temple, where he brings his message home to the very nerve centre of Jewish religious identity. It is a challenge that seems calculated to court controversy. Amid the teeming crowds and the heightened atmosphere of a major festival, this assertive move provokes both astonishment and fury.

The polemical debate that follows does not make for easy reading. On one level, we might imagine a witty and good-natured intellectual exchange between traditionalist and radical exponents of the law. But there is a darker and more threatening level of argument that Jesus does not flinch from naming: 'Why are you looking for an opportunity to kill me?'

It can be deeply shocking to recognize the violent undercurrents that crackle beneath the surface of seemingly polite religious debate. Anyone who is bold enough, when necessary, to challenge vested interests of prestige and power must learn to expect some ferocious reactions. Jesus steps forward as someone who is willing to speak truth to power. He is not afraid to own his God-given authority. Nor is he naïve about the conflict that will inevitably ensue. Do we share his courage?

COLLECT

Almighty God,
you show to those who are in error the light of your truth,
that they may return to the way of righteousness:
grant to all those who are admitted
    into the fellowship of Christ's religion,
that they may reject those things
    that are contrary to their profession,
and follow all such things as are agreeable to the same;
through our Lord Jesus Christ,
who is alive and reigns with you,
in the unity of the Holy Spirit,
one God, now and for ever.

Reflection by **Margaret Whipp**

Psalms 3, **25** *or* 96, **97**, 100
Jeremiah 10.17-24
John 7.25-36

Saturday 6 March

John 7.25-36

'I know him' (v.29)

Most modern languages use different words to describe forms of knowledge. There is an objective knowledge, *knowing about* someone or something, which is quite different from the intimate, subjective *knowledge of* someone through personal relationship.

Jesus takes his opponents to task over their woefully shallow knowledge of God. They murmur and quibble over points of abstruse interpretation, whilst failing to recognize the embodiment of grace and truth that stands right before their eyes. Page after page, the evangelist attests to Jesus' intimate relationship with God. Though no one has seen God directly, Jesus is 'the only Son, who is close to the Father's heart, who has made him known' (John 1.18).

All true knowledge is based on relationship. Jesus is secure in this personal knowledge of the Father. We may project all our fears and prejudices onto a distorted, idolatrous image of God. But genuine knowledge comes through humble seeking, and loving, and serving. This was the source of Jesus' radical freedom: and it can be ours as well.

A great prayer by Saint Augustine addresses God as 'the light of the minds that know thee, the life of the souls that love thee, and the strength of the wills that serve thee'. Through Jesus, we too can pray St Augustine's words: 'Help us so to know thee that we may truly love thee, so to love thee that we may fully serve thee, whose service is perfect freedom.'

Almighty God,
by the prayer and discipline of Lent
may we enter into the mystery of Christ's sufferings,
and by following in his Way
come to share in his glory;
through Jesus Christ our Lord.

COLLECT

Monday 8 March

Psalms **5**, 7 *or* **98**, 99, 101
Jeremiah 11.1-17
John 7.37-52

John 7.37-52

'Let anyone who is thirsty come to me' (v.37)

The Festival of Booths (or Tabernacles) was a sort of Harvest Thanksgiving since it celebrated the gathering in of the crops and fruit. It went on a long time. Huts were built made of branches (the booths or tabernacles of the title), recalling the temporary dwellings of the Israelites in their 40 years in the wilderness.

John doesn't explain any of this. Nor does he tell us about the custom of pouring water over the altar, a sign of God's promise that he would pour out his Spirit on his people. When Jesus speaks of quenching the thirst of the spiritually parched, he indicates that the promise at the heart of this great festival was being fulfilled in him, from whom would flow 'rivers of living water'.

Most readers of John's Gospel down the centuries would not have known the connection between these words of Jesus and customs at the Feast of Booths. It isn't necessary to know it. The reader of the Gospel only needs to recognize what it is to be spiritually dry and parched. Without that recognition, there is not much that Jesus can do for us. The human body cannot live long without water. Spiritual lifelessness is the consequence of not seeking the streams of living water Jesus promises us. This may be a particular danger for those of us well established in the faith who may neglect gradually the source of a healthy spiritual life.

COLLECT

Almighty God,
whose most dear Son went not up to joy
    but first he suffered pain,
and entered not into glory before he was crucified:
mercifully grant that we, walking in the way of the cross,
may find it none other than the way of life and peace;
through Jesus Christ your Son our Lord,
who is alive and reigns with you,
in the unity of the Holy Spirit,
one God, now and for ever.

Reflection by **Graham James**

Psalms 6, **9** *or* **106*** (*or* 103)   **Tuesday 9 March**
Jeremiah 11.18 – 12.6
John 7.53 – 8.11

John 7.53 – 8.11

'Neither do I condemn you' (v.11)

This famous encounter between Jesus and the woman taken in adultery is not primarily about sexual infidelity. Any temptation to cast Jesus as a twenty-first-century liberal on sexual matters is a mistake. It's his refusal to condemn this woman who has sinned against the law of Moses that is the focus of the story.

A great crowd has gathered, keen to hear Jesus. We are probably in the outer Court of the Women in the Temple since that was where anyone could listen to religious teachers. Scribes and Pharisees arrive with the presumably distraught and dishevelled woman in tow. (There's no mention of the man involved.) She is being used (and abused) to set a trap for Jesus. If he fails to condemn her to be stoned, he would be denying the Mosaic law. But if he does so, he would be usurping the Roman authorities' exclusive right to impose a death penalty.

Instead of debating the issue, Jesus simply invites anyone who is without sin to cast the first stone. The whole crowd gradually dissolves. No one has condemned her, and neither does Jesus. He has not come to condemn but to save the world (John 3.17).

Even the briefest review of the tabloid press or social media shows that condemnation remains commonplace today. Condemnation is eternal death. The gospel is a protest against such ready condemnation. Are we able to rid ourselves of this deadly error?

Eternal God,
give us insight
to discern your will for us,
to give up what harms us,
and to seek the perfection we are promised
in Jesus Christ our Lord.

COLLECT

Reflection by **Graham James**   25

Wednesday 10 March

John 8.12-30

'I am the light of the world' (v.12)

At the Feast of Booths (or Tabernacles), four great lamps were lit in the temple, in the Court of the Women. The blaze on the Temple Mount could be seen for miles. In the Psalms, both the law ('a lamp to my feet' Psalm 119) and the Lord himself ('my light and my salvation' Psalm 27) were sources of illumination. The imagery was familiar and powerful.

For Jesus to speak of himself as 'the light of the world' was thus the boldest of claims. He was claiming to be sent from the Father to lead the people of God out of darkness, and also to be the authentic interpreter of the law and the prophets. From this point in John's Gospel, the enemies of Jesus become more vocal. What seems to us a gentle and attractive 'I am' saying of Jesus was, for his accusers, one of the most pernicious.

Lights have been used in most forms of Christian worship down the centuries, particularly candles. The symbolism of candles has never lost its attraction even in the age of electricity. Perhaps it's because a candle is a living flame. A living flame needs oxygen, just like human beings. As it burns, a candle is gradually dying. The light of the world, drawing the same air as the people he comes to save, is on the way to his death.

COLLECT

Almighty God,
whose most dear Son went not up to joy
    but first he suffered pain,
and entered not into glory before he was crucified:
mercifully grant that we, walking in the way of the cross,
may find it none other than the way of life and peace;
through Jesus Christ your Son our Lord,
who is alive and reigns with you,
in the unity of the Holy Spirit,
one God, now and for ever.

| *Reflection by* **Graham** James

Psalms **56**, 57 *or* 113, **115**
Jeremiah 14
John 8.31-47

John 8.31-47

'... he [the devil] is a liar and the father of lies' (v.44)

Jesus charges some of his fellow Jews with not following Abraham but doing the bidding of the devil and father of lies. His words were employed by the Nazis to demonize all Jews. Yet John's Gospel is clear that there were many Jews who believed in Jesus. Jesus declares that his real opponent is the devil, the great deceiver who appears to be telling the truth when he is lying and leads people to perdition.

The Greek word for devil, *diabolos*, means 'slanderer'. The law of slander in most countries applies at the most serious end of false accusation. The alternative translation 'backbiter' brings it a bit closer to our own behaviours. Once I heard someone render *diabolos* as 'fault-finding spirit'. Few of us seem to avoid fault-finding. We tend to find fault behind people's backs – a very different thing from constructive criticism. Sometimes we do it to make ourselves feel superior, but it is destructive of trust and truth. We are much more likely to see the speck of dust in someone else's eye while ignoring the boulders in our own.

Jesus speaks of the devil as the father of lies. He also speaks about the truth setting us free. What about making this a day – or even a week – free of fault-finding? If we escape the clutches of the father of lies, we will travel on the way to the truth which sets us free.

> Eternal God,
> give us insight
> to discern your will for us,
> to give up what harms us,
> and to seek the perfection we are promised
> in Jesus Christ our Lord.

COLLECT

Lent

Friday 12 March

Psalm **22** *or* **139**
Jeremiah 15.10-end
John 8.48-end

John 8.48-end
'... before Abraham was, I am' (v.58)

The idea that our identity is not fixed but discovered is a relatively recent one. In relation to gender, there are new possibilities for change, at least for some people. But there is nothing new in questions of identity proving controversial, especially when they relate to our parentage. It was through DNA that Justin Welby, the Archbishop of Canterbury, discovered his father was Anthony Montague-Browne, once Winston Churchill's private secretary. Without downplaying the significance of this discovery, the Archbishop used the opportunity to say that his genetic make-up was not the primary factor in the person he believed himself to be. 'My identity is founded in who I am in Christ', he said.

Our identity is shaped by a range of characteristics – gender, race, family, nationality, culture and belief among them. In today's passage from John's Gospel, Jesus claims to have existed before Abraham, identifying himself with the God of heaven and earth in his eternal being. His words seem an unmistakeable allusion to God's own self-description in Exodus 3: 'I am who I am.' Thus, Jesus reveals his own identity. If what he is saying is not true, he has committed the greatest blasphemy. What gives us our identity? When we are in Christ, we do not throw off the complete range of characteristics that make each of us unique. But what weight do we give them? Would we agree with the words of the Archbishop?

COLLECT

Almighty God,
whose most dear Son went not up to joy
    but first he suffered pain,
and entered not into glory before he was crucified:
mercifully grant that we, walking in the way of the cross,
may find it none other than the way of life and peace;
through Jesus Christ your Son our Lord,
who is alive and reigns with you,
in the unity of the Holy Spirit,
one God, now and for ever.

Reflection by **Graham James**

Psalm **31** *or* 120, **121**, 122
Jeremiah 16.10 – 17.4
John 9.1-17

John 9.1-17
'Go, wash in the pool of Siloam' (v.7)

Jesus, 'the light of the world', now gives sight to a man born blind. More than that, the previously blind man, gradually comes to see who Jesus is. He sees more than many who have never wanted for sight.

My maternal grandmother became blind from glaucoma shortly before I was born. She was a faithful follower of Jesus Christ. Sometimes she heard the preachers in her chapel suggest that the healing miracles of Jesus, including when he gave sight to the blind, depended on the faith and trust of the one who was healed. And yet she, who had no shortage of faith and trust, had become blind. What did she lack? It was certainly not spiritual sight.

This chapter of John's Gospel was a comfort to her. The blind man doesn't even ask to be given sight. Jesus heals him before they exchange a word. He does so by mixing the dust of the earth (out of which we are all created) with his saliva (thought to be a precious source of life in the ancient world). And then the man washes in the pool of Siloam – in water from well beyond Jerusalem, thanks to Hezekiah's long tunnel. The creator of all, the light of the world, the fount of living water – they all give the blind man his spiritual as well as physical sight. What signs of God will we be able to see today?

Eternal God,
give us insight
to discern your will for us,
to give up what harms us,
and to seek the perfection we are promised
in Jesus Christ our Lord.

COLLECT

Reflection by **Graham James** | 29

Monday 15 March   Psalms 70, **77** or 123, 124, 125, **126**
Jeremiah 17.5-18
John 9.18-end

John 9.18-end
'His parents … were afraid' (v.22)

The blind man's parents make an appearance as their son is being questioned about Jesus. What do they know about how he received his sight? They are evasive, claiming they don't know who opened their son's eyes. They don't want to get involved. Their boy is old enough to speak for himself, so they prefer to keep out of the controversy that surrounds him. The Gospel writer suggests they feared expulsion from the synagogue and the community if they testified to Jesus as someone working with God's authority.

This encounter with the blind man's parents may seem a minor detail in a bigger story, but it probably had significance for some of the first readers of John's Gospel. Jews who followed Christ knew what it was to be expelled from their synagogues for believing Jesus was the Messiah. Some of them experienced their families standing aside or even betraying them. Those whose eyes were opened to see the truth about Jesus found the cost of discipleship meant being cast out from their community, and sometimes from their family as well.

Many Christians today know what it is to experience indifference or hostility from their families. Some are excluded and even betrayed. Discipleship can be a lonely experience.

What's been the greatest cost you have experienced in following Jesus Christ?

COLLECT | Merciful Lord,
absolve your people from their offences,
that through your bountiful goodness
we may all be delivered from the chains of those sins
which by our frailty we have committed;
grant this, heavenly Father,
for Jesus Christ's sake, our blessed Lord and Saviour,
who is alive and reigns with you,
in the unity of the Holy Spirit,
one God, now and for ever.

Reflection by **Graham James**

Psalms 54, **79** *or* **132**, 133
Jeremiah 18.1-12
John 10.1-10

Tuesday 16 March

John 10.1-10
'... the shepherd of the sheep' (v.2)

Pope Francis has said that the shepherds of the Roman Catholic Church should have 'the smell of the sheep' about them. He calls his bishops and clergy to immerse themselves in the lives of the people they serve.

Shepherds live closely with their sheep. In recent years, James Rebanks, a shepherd in the Lake District in the UK, has attracted tens of thousands of followers to his Twitter account describing his daily life and work. His book *The Shepherd's Life* was an unexpected bestseller. He is the son of a shepherd, and his father was the son of a shepherd too. It's in his bones. His descriptions of the lambing season and the hard work of winter months show that he smells of his sheep.

Few people have direct experience of shepherding, but it does not take much imagination to understand this imagery. Even so, the Gospel writer suggests that those listening to Jesus were slow to catch on. That's surprising, since the relationship between God and his people was frequently expressed in ancient Israel as one of sheep and shepherd, as in Psalm 23, 'The Lord is my shepherd'.

Sometimes pastoral imagery is used in the Church almost exclusively in relation to official ministers. They should certainly smell of the sheep. But most of us have others who fall within our care, and should know our voice and our concern for them. To whom will we be shepherds today?

Merciful Lord,
you know our struggle to serve you:
when sin spoils our lives
and overshadows our hearts,
come to our aid
and turn us back to you again;
through Jesus Christ our Lord.

COLLECT

Wednesday 17 March

John 10.11-21

'... there will be one flock, one shepherd' (v.16)

This vision of the good shepherd drawing everyone into one flock comes after we have been told that the blind man to whom Jesus gave sight was driven out of his community (John 9.34). He was expelled because he would not condemn Jesus for giving him his sight on the sabbath. (Even a mighty work done on the sabbath contravened the law of Moses, so the scribes and Pharisees claimed.)

Jesus draws a contrast between religious teachers concerned to keep the purity of their group, whatever the human casualties, and his own desire to draw in 'other sheep who do not belong to this fold'. He does not say who these other sheep are, but early readers of John's Gospel would have included many gentiles, who may have applied these words to themselves. It's likely, however, that the words of the prophet Ezekiel provide the context here. The prophet condemns the religious leaders of his day. God himself will have to come and be the people's shepherd. 'I myself will be the shepherd of my sheep ... I will seek the lost ... bring back the strayed ... bind up the injured .... strengthen the weak' (Ezekiel 34.15,16). The whole course of the ministry of Jesus has been shaped by these priorities. It has brought vehement opposition. The question John poses his readers is 'Whose side are you on?', though he is too subtle to put it quite so crudely.

COLLECT

Merciful Lord,
absolve your people from their offences,
that through your bountiful goodness
we may all be delivered from the chains of those sins
which by our frailty we have committed;
grant this, heavenly Father,
for Jesus Christ's sake, our blessed Lord and Saviour,
who is alive and reigns with you,
in the unity of the Holy Spirit,
one God, now and for ever.

| *Reflection by* **Graham James**

Thursday 18 March

John 10.22-end

'If you are the Messiah, tell us plainly' (v.24)

Some people see God in many places – in the dawn of a new day, a forgiving word, the birth of a child, an act of self-sacrifice or being in love. Others experience the very same things but see no evidence that God exists at all.

A similar dynamic is found here when Jesus is asked to say plainly if he is the Messiah. He has already claimed to be the light of the world, the good shepherd and the bread of life. Jesus has given sight to the blind, fed five thousand people, healed the son of a royal official, and cured a lame man at the pool of Bethesda. If they do not believe his words, he says, then surely his works speak for themselves. How could he have spoken and acted more plainly?

John notes, almost in passing, that it is the Festival of Dedication, known also as the Festival of Lights. It celebrates the rededication of the temple a century and a half earlier following its desecration. It's a time when many lamps are lit. In Jesus, the light of the world has come and is in plain sight. And yet many refuse to see.

The accusers of Jesus may not want to see who he is, perhaps because he confounds their expectations of who the Messiah should be or what he should do. What expectations may blind us to seeing God plainly in our lives today?

Merciful Lord,
you know our struggle to serve you:
when sin spoils our lives
and overshadows our hearts,
come to our aid
and turn us back to you again;
through Jesus Christ our Lord.

COLLECT

Reflection by **Graham James** | 33

Friday 19 March

Joseph of Nazareth

Psalms 25, 147.1-12
Isaiah 11.1-10
Matthew 13.54-end

Isaiah 11.1-10

'A shoot shall come out from the stock of Jesse' (v.1)

Isaiah 11 begins with an eloquent vision of a kingdom of justice, righteousness and wisdom, with a ruler whose 'delight will be in the fear of the Lord'. The people of Israel have been faithless and have lost their king. Isaiah expects renewal to come when a new shoot emerges from the line of Jesse, the father of King David.

Centuries later, Matthew's Gospel begins by recalling how the lineage of Joseph, the husband of Mary, can be traced back to David and Jesse and even to Abraham. Despite the belief in the virgin birth and Joseph's status as guardian or foster-father of Jesus, Joseph's ancestry is treated as highly significant. He has his own place in enabling Jesus to proclaim the kingdom of peace anticipated in Isaiah's vision.

Joseph's support for Mary and protection of his son are central to the birth narratives and the early life of Jesus. Yet he fades from the story and has not always been given the profile he deserves in the Church. For example, it was only in 1962 that his name was added to the long list of saints mentioned in the Canon of the Mass in the Roman Catholic Church. Perhaps this makes Joseph a suitable saint for our own age when in Western societies the role of fathers is sometimes contested, unclear or undervalued.

COLLECT

God our Father,
who from the family of your servant David
raised up Joseph the carpenter
to be the guardian of your incarnate Son
and husband of the Blessed Virgin Mary:
give us grace to follow him
in faithful obedience to your commands;
through Jesus Christ your Son our Lord,
who is alive and reigns with you,
in the unity of the Holy Spirit,
one God, now and for ever.

Reflection by **Graham James**

Psalm **32** *or* **147**
Jeremiah 20.7-end
John 11.17-27

Saturday 20 March

John 11.17-27

'... if you had been here my brother would not have died' (v.21)

I once visited a priest whose wife had died two days previously. He told me he had already worked through the stages of bereavement and come to acceptance. It seemed unlikely in 48 hours. Then his wife's sister arrived. He told her that if she had come earlier, his wife might not have died. I felt rather relieved that his grief was still so raw. The tears flowed.

Martha's grief is raw too. We know her and Mary from Luke's Gospel where Mary is the one who sits listening to Jesus while Martha rushes around doing the household chores. Here we learn they have a brother Lazarus who has died. Mary sits at home mourning. Martha, by contrast, is out to greet Jesus. She blames him for not being there to prevent Lazarus' death. But Martha still hopes Jesus can do something. She believes in the resurrection on the last day. That was common enough in Judaism at the time. Jesus tells her, 'I am the resurrection and the life'. The light of the world is also life for all eternity. Through him anyone can discover what it is to live abundantly. It's with her bereavement still raw that Martha makes the fullest profession of faith found in John's Gospel: 'You are the Messiah, the Son of God, the one coming into the world.' If she had suppressed her grief, would she have made this life-changing discovery?

COLLECT

Merciful Lord,
absolve your people from their offences,
that through your bountiful goodness
we may all be delivered from the chains of those sins
which by our frailty we have committed;
grant this, heavenly Father,
for Jesus Christ's sake, our blessed Lord and Saviour,
who is alive and reigns with you,
in the unity of the Holy Spirit,
one God, now and for ever.

Reflection by **Graham James** | 35

Monday 22 March

Psalms **73**, 121 *or* 1, 2, 3
Jeremiah 21.1-10
John 11.28-44

John 11.28-44
'Did I not tell you ...' (v.40)

Today's passage is charged with emotional intensity. Echoes of Martha's remarkable declaration that Jesus is the Messiah in verse 27 mingle with grief following Lazarus' death. His sisters are deeply distressed, and angry with Jesus for arriving late. Their loss is heightened by the presence of other mourners, and we sense the gentle bustle of activity that often accompanies major life events. Into this mix Jesus' own anguish spills over and he begins to weep. Then there is talk of opening the tomb, Martha's anxiety about the body's decomposition and finally the dramatic emergence of Lazarus.

Throughout, the ordinary and extraordinary are held side by side. Jesus' divinity and humanity are present in equal measure. Mary and Martha's touching faith in Jesus doesn't diminish their frustration. Jesus himself is overcome with the sadness of loss, and perhaps his own imminent suffering and death, just moments before he calls Lazarus out.

Life and death are both in the balance as we are reminded that the holding together of apparently impossible contradictions is so often the way of faith. In the Persian calendar, yesterday was Nowruz – New Year. I remember as a child growing up in Iran how it wasn't unusual for the Church community to celebrate the Nowruz season at the start of each Spring, with its promise of new life and renewal, while at the same time marking a solemn event in the Christian calendar, such as Good Friday. The experience was and is a permanent reminder that in life there is always death and in times of greatest sorrow there is always hope of resurrection.

COLLECT

Most merciful God,
who by the death and resurrection of your Son Jesus Christ
delivered and saved the world:
grant that by faith in him who suffered on the cross
we may triumph in the power of his victory;
through Jesus Christ your Son our Lord,
who is alive and reigns with you,
in the unity of the Holy Spirit,
one God, now and for ever.

36 | *Reflection by* **Guli Francis-Dehqani**

Psalms **35**, 123 *or* **5**, 6 (8)
Jeremiah 22.1-5, 13-19
John 11.45-end

Tuesday 23 March

John 11.45-end

'... and he remained there with the disciples' (v.54)

The chief priests and Pharisees are fearful of Jesus' impact on the crowds and of potential political consequences. Caiaphas is frightened for his own status and position. Even Jesus, it seems, experiences fear; he's lying low, refusing to emerge in public, not yet ready to face the end.

Fear is a healthy human instinct. It acts as a warning against imminent dangers, ensuring we protect ourselves and others. We teach children to be wary of fire, careful chopping vegetables, mindful crossing the road – a gentle instilling of fear in the face of possible dangers. Talking with my teenage son recently about what he might do if he were mugged, my advice was, 'don't be brave, give them your wallet and run'. In other words, be sensibly fearful and act accordingly.

Yet sometimes we must rise above our fears with unwavering determination. In some parts of the world, Christians face physical danger and persecution, which many meet with extraordinary courage and bravery. In other parts of the world, fear emerges from the Church's increasing marginalization. This is the fear of loss of influence, of irrelevance and eventual extinction. This kind of fear corrodes and creates the illusion that the future of the Church is dependent on us. In reality, the future is in God's hands. Our calling, whatever our context, is to resist fear, be faithful in the knowledge of God's constant presence, and to love without ceasing.

Gracious Father,
you gave up your Son
out of love for the world:
lead us to ponder the mysteries of his passion,
that we may know eternal peace
through the shedding of our Saviour's blood,
Jesus Christ our Lord.

COLLECT

Reflection by **Guli Francis-Dehqani**

Wednesday 24 March

Psalms **55**, 124 *or* **119.1-32**
Jeremiah 22.20 – 23.8
John 12.1-11

John 12.1-11

'The house was filled with the fragrance of the perfume' (v.3)

I imagine Mary's actions in anointing Jesus' feet to have been entirely spontaneous – an outpouring of great love – feelings of the heart overwhelming logic of the head. This shocking yet exquisitely beautiful offering is in direct contrast to Judas' self-righteous anger, justified with perfectly reasonable arguments about how the money could have been spent on the poor. The story is a reminder that the realm of faith is never fully explainable by the intellect but demands a response, beyond mere reason, from the very core of our soul.

But this story also confronts our sometimes comfortable complacency. It challenges us to take risks and to stand up for others. Mary took a monumental risk. What she did was not only wastefully extravagant but well beyond conventional behaviour for a woman. It would hardly have been surprising had Jesus himself chastised her. And yet she took a risk to show how much she loved him.

Then, in a wonderful gesture of solidarity, Jesus *stood up for Mary*. 'Leave her alone', he said in response to Judas' reprimand. Mary was accused unfairly, and Jesus, who could so easily have remained silent, came to her defence.

When was the last time you took a risk for your faith, doing what was right instead of what was easiest? When was the last time you spoke up for someone else, when it would have been so much easier to bow your head in silence?

COLLECT

Most merciful God,
who by the death and resurrection of your Son Jesus Christ
delivered and saved the world:
grant that by faith in him who suffered on the cross
we may triumph in the power of his victory;
through Jesus Christ your Son our Lord,
who is alive and reigns with you,
in the unity of the Holy Spirit,
one God, now and for ever.

Reflection by **Guli Francis-Dehqani**

Psalms 111, 113
1 Samuel 2.1-10
Romans 5.12-end

Thursday 25 March
Annunciation of Our Lord to the Blessed Virgin Mary

Romans 5.12-end

'... the many will be made righteous' (v.19)

Today, we celebrate the feast of the Annunciation – a foretelling of the incarnation and the announcement by Angel Gabriel to Mary that she would give birth to God's son. The Bible passage is Paul's theological underpinning of why Christ's coming was necessary. With the events of Holy Week just around the corner, these verses provide a link between the birth narratives and those that tell of Jesus' death.

Paul's is a dense thesis in which Adam and Christ are compared, one bringing sin to the world through disobedience and the other reconciliation through righteousness. Adam and Christ represent choices about what kind of existence we desire: one that ends in death or one that leads to eternal life. If it is the latter, we must journey into next week when Christ's obedience will take him to the cross, from where he will transform violence to gentleness, hatred to love and death to life.

The gift of life, Paul stresses, is free and for the taking. It is an invitation that we can only accept in trust and faith, and it doesn't promise an easy path. Gabriel's message to Mary was also an invitation to which she responded 'yes'. Her journey was full of suffering, but still today Mary is a reminder of how often we encounter Christ most forcefully when we are most wounded and it is then we discover the true value of the new life he offers.

COLLECT

We beseech you, O Lord,
pour your grace into our hearts,
that as we have known the incarnation of your Son Jesus Christ
by the message of an angel,
so by his cross and passion
we may be brought to the glory of his resurrection;
through Jesus Christ your Son our Lord,
who is alive and reigns with you,
in the unity of the Holy Spirit,
one God, now and for ever.

Reflection by **Guli Francis-Dehqani** | 39

Friday 26 March

Psalms 22, 126 *or* 17, 19
Jeremiah 24
John 12.20-36*a*

John 12.20-36*a*

'... it is for this reason that I have come to this hour' (v.27)

Jesus associates his impending death with glory: 'The hour has come for the Son of Man to be glorified' – an odd juxtaposition, underscoring the upside-down world of God's economy where failure and suffering are redeemed. Christ's moment of greatest suffering is to be his moment of greatest glory as love and gentleness overcome hatred and violence.

Approaching his death, Jesus doesn't speak of how to ensure his legacy continues. He talks instead of a seed dying before it bears fruit. This reminds me of the words of the early Christian author Tertullian: 'the blood of the martyrs is the seed of the Church' – death leading to new growth. Let's not romanticize the reality, but this often seems to be the experience of the persecuted Church – that through times of trial and suffering comes a deepening of faith, new insights into the meaning of the cross and hope for the future.

There is much talk at present, in the West especially, of how to safeguard the future of a shrinking Church. It is right and proper that we take seriously our calling to proclaim the faith afresh in each generation and pass it on to the next. But in the process there is a danger that we might just miss something profound about fruit coming only once the seed has died. It is a painful truth to contemplate, but what might you in your context need to allow to die in order that something new might blossom?

COLLECT

Most merciful God,
who by the death and resurrection of your Son Jesus Christ
delivered and saved the world:
grant that by faith in him who suffered on the cross
we may triumph in the power of his victory;
through Jesus Christ your Son our Lord,
who is alive and reigns with you,
in the unity of the Holy Spirit,
one God, now and for ever.

Reflection by **Guli Francis-Dehqani**

Psalms **23**, 127 *or* 20, 21, **23**   **Saturday 27 March**
Jeremiah 25.1-14
John 12.36*b*-end

John 12.36*b*-end

'... for they loved human glory more than the glory that comes from God' (v.43)

John marks the end of Jesus' public ministry with the brief statement that 'he departed and hid from them'. The time for telling stories and parables, for teaching and performing miracles is over, and the people won't see Jesus again until after his arrest. In human terms, his efforts had failed. After all he'd said and done, the people did not believe in him. It must have hurt. There must have been a part of Jesus that had hoped the suffering wouldn't be needed. That through skill and effort and commitment he would manage to convince people of the need to repent and believe.

If Jesus was, as we believe, fully human (as well as fully God), then his need for worldly affirmation will have been real and strong. Most of us are familiar with the feeling; we look for it again and again – to be noticed, successful, wealthy, influential. We may tell ourselves it's because we want to do good, and at our best there may be something of that. But in truth, this craving for human affirmation comes from a need to prove ourselves – to convince others, and ourselves, that we are worthwhile, valued and, ultimately, loved. Jesus' acceptance of his calling demonstrates that all we really need is to embrace our ultimate identity as beloved of God – those who are loved not because of what we achieve but simply because of who we are.

Gracious Father,
you gave up your Son
out of love for the world:
lead us to ponder the mysteries of his passion,
that we may know eternal peace
through the shedding of our Saviour's blood,
Jesus Christ our Lord.

COLLECT

Reflection by **Guli Francis-Dehqani**   41

Monday 29 March

Monday of Holy Week

Psalm 41
Lamentations 1.1-12*a*
Luke 22.1-23

Luke 22.1-23

'When the hour came ...' (v.14)

Fear, betrayal and conspiracy are themes that set the mood in today's passage as we begin the journey through Holy Week. Jesus must have sensed that events were overtaking him, that things had moved to the point of no return and the final outcome was looking grim. I know when my anxieties are really heightened, normal routines escape me. I struggle to think straight or make good decisions. The idea of eating, never mind preparing a meal to share with others, is appalling. Yet that's exactly what Jesus does. He calmly carries on with his plans, arranges a meal with his disciples and prepares them for what is to come by establishing the central act of remembrance whereby we still encounter him centuries on every time we partake in Holy Communion.

What is so striking about these verses is that although people are closing in and Jesus appears to be at the mercy of others, he in fact remains in charge, totally in control, setting the agenda and the pace. The point is, of course, that he wasn't entering this phase unprepared. Jesus' entire life was founded on securing his relationship with his heavenly father. And this gave him confidence to focus his thinking and steadily follow his calling.

For us to enter our times of trial with composure, we too need to have done the groundwork, establishing a life based on prayer and reliance on God.

COLLECT

Almighty and everlasting God,
who in your tender love towards the human race
    sent your Son our Saviour Jesus Christ
to take upon him our flesh
and to suffer death upon the cross:
grant that we may follow the example of his patience and humility,
and also be made partakers of his resurrection;
through Jesus Christ your Son our Lord,
who is alive and reigns with you,
in the unity of the Holy Spirit,
one God, now and for ever.

42   *Reflection by* **Guli Francis-Dehqani**

Psalm 27
Lamentations 3.1-18
Luke 22. [24-38] 39-53

Tuesday 30 March
Tuesday of Holy Week

Luke 22. [24-38] 39-53

'Pray that you may not come into the time of trial' (v.40)

Today, we begin to get a proper sense of the extent of Jesus' agony. As doubt creeps in and fear grips him, he descends to the depths of despair. 'Remove this cup from me', he implores and, as he prays earnestly, sweat pours off him like droplets of blood. It's a vivid picture of dread and terror. And then ... they come to arrest him. How tempting it must have been to allow the disciples to protect him with their swords and to flee to a place of safety under the cover of darkness. Instead, Jesus embraces the suffering that lies ahead, admonishes the disciple who has struck the slave and heals his ear.

It's not until an orange is squeezed that you know if the juice is sweet or sour. It's not until any of us is gravely tested that we'll know the extent of our faithfulness and obedience. It is sobering to think of the host of martyrs down the centuries who have remained true, refusing to deny their faith, even to the point of death; those who have refused to flee but bravely stood up for truth in the face of injustice.

As we give thanks for those who have gone before, we pray for Christians persecuted around the world today and we pause to consider for a moment: 'What would I do if they came for me?'

COLLECT

True and humble king,
hailed by the crowd as Messiah:
grant us the faith to know you and love you,
that we may be found beside you
on the way of the cross,
which is the path of glory.

Reflection by **Guli Francis-Dehqani**   43

Wednesday 31 March
Wednesday of Holy Week

Psalm 102 [*or* 102.1-18]
Wisdom 1.16 – 2.1; 2.12-22
or Jeremiah 11.18-20
Luke 22.54-end

Luke 22.54-end
'Then Peter remembered' (v.61)

The night before writing this, I visited a prison in my area where inmates were performing their own poetry and music following a rehabilitation workshop. A line from one of the pieces has remained with me: 'I've stolen, I've lied, I've been deceitful; I've done all these things but I've never lost hope'. A touching portrayal of what it's like to recognize when we've sunk to our lowest while knowing too that it doesn't need to be the end; that it can be a turning point and the beginning of the path to renewal.

That's how we meet Peter today. The crowing cockerel and a look from Jesus trigger the memory of his brash confidence just days before, and with it comes the devastating realization of how badly he's failed. This could have been the end for Peter. He might well have walked away – fled and returned to his fishing nets and the safety of his old life. Instead, the incident becomes a defining moment, which brought him eventually to the reassertion of his loyalty, his restoration by the risen Jesus and the calling to become shepherd of the flock.

And there is the challenge for each of us. After we fail (as we surely will) and after weeping bitter tears of regret, which direction will we choose to travel? The short road to self-pity and defeatism or the long road through forgiveness to healing and recovery?

COLLECT

Almighty and everlasting God,
who in your tender love towards the human race
    sent your Son our Saviour Jesus Christ
to take upon him our flesh
and to suffer death upon the cross:
grant that we may follow the example of his patience and humility,
and also be made partakers of his resurrection;
through Jesus Christ your Son our Lord,
who is alive and reigns with you,
in the unity of the Holy Spirit,
one God, now and for ever.

Reflection by **Guli Francis-Dehqani**

Psalms 42, 43
Leviticus 16.2-24
Luke 23.1-25

Thursday I April
Maundy Thursday

Luke 23.1-25

'... but Jesus gave him no answer' (v.9)

One of the things I find most difficult to deal with in life is when I feel I've been treated unfairly. I'm talking here about the everyday small injustices we encounter, often over relatively insignificant matters that nonetheless, in the moment, leave us feeling powerless, hurt and humiliated. Times when we've been misrepresented, wrongly accused or just treated a little shoddily and every fibre of our being is bristling with anger and our instinct is to lash out in response.

Now, I'm a passionate advocate of Christians speaking out and acting for justice in situations of abuse and persecution or where a crime is being committed. And yet there is also something in the Christian story (and at the heart of today's reading) about the place of humility – of knowing that sometimes the better response is to remain undefended, acknowledge the pain, find it in our heart to forgive and move on – to mend relationships rather than damage them further.

Jesus, who not long ago had angrily cast out the moneylenders from the temple, now stands silent before Pilate and Herod. And as he does so, he demonstrates the extraordinary courage and conviction needed to take this stance. In his demeanour we don't see weakness but rather a profound show of strength. May God grant us the wisdom to know when to take action against the injustices we experience and when to remain silent.

True and humble king,
hailed by the crowd as Messiah:
grant us the faith to know you and love you,
that we may be found beside you
on the way of the cross,
which is the path of glory.

COLLECT

Reflection by **Guli Francis-Dehqani**

Friday 2 April
Good Friday

Psalm 69
Genesis 22.1-18
John 19.38-end
or Hebrews 10.1-10

Hebrews 10.1-10
'... make perfect those who approach' (v.1)

I'm eternally grateful to my parents for their gift of unconditional love. However guilty I was at times of behaving badly or causing them hurt, I never doubted that I was loved; I never had to prove myself worthy of their devotion. Despite my many failings, their love helped form and shape me, giving me security, confidence and, perhaps most importantly, insights into forgiveness and compassion.

And in the language of faith, that is what Paul reminds us of in today's reading, and it is what lies at the heart of Good Friday. Today, guilt is overcome by love. Jesus' unswerving obedience and faithfulness even to death on a cross releases us from perpetual guilt (which required regular sacrifices), and instead we are embraced by unconditional love. Today, the law makes way for grace. Jesus becomes the *final sacrifice* – once and for all – and we are beckoned towards freedom. No more guilt, no more sacrifices and no more need to prove ourselves worthy of God's love. That is the extraordinary message of Good Friday that our wounded world is in such great need of hearing.

As we stand at the foot of the cross, so we discover our true identity as children of God, loved unconditionally, soaked in grace, no longer burdened by sin and guilt. Here, in the outstretched arms of Christ, we find healing for our pain and, despite the darkness, the glimmer of new beginnings.

COLLECT

Almighty Father,
look with mercy on this your family
for which our Lord Jesus Christ was content to be betrayed
    and given up into the hands of sinners
    and to suffer death upon the cross;
who is alive and glorified with you and the Holy Spirit,
one God, now and for ever.

| *Reflection by* **Guli Francis-Dehqani**

Psalm 142
Hosea 6.1-6
John 2.18-22

Saturday 3 April
Easter Eve

John 2.18-22

'... in three days I will raise it up' (v.19)

Today's verses follow on from Jesus' cleansing of the temple. The people are demanding an explanation about his actions and his reply comes in the form both of a riddle and a parable. In Jewish tradition, 'after three days' or 'on the third day' was a phrase used to indicate a length of time before God would deliver the people from their troubles. Three days denotes a turning point towards something new and better. It suggests, also, a period of waiting – it isn't now or tomorrow, but after three days. There is need for patience and fortitude.

In this passage, God is relocated from a place to a person – from being present in the temple to being present in the body of Jesus. We know that our access to God is now through a *relationship* with the person of Christ and that we cannot restrict God to a place or building. But however much we *believe* this to be true, sometimes we struggle to *feel* it. Sometimes God feels very far and we are swamped by darkness and silence. Sometimes we are powerless to change circumstances as we would like. Well, today is the day when our doubt and emptiness and helplessness is honoured in the Church calendar; when we sit with our pain and dwell with our uncertainty, unable to fix things or speed them up, but instead clinging on until 'the third day' when all we will revealed.

Grant, Lord,
that we who are baptized into the death
of your Son our Saviour Jesus Christ
may continually put to death our evil desires
and be buried with him;
and that through the grave and gate of death
we may pass to our joyful resurrection;
through his merits,
who died and was buried and rose again for us,
your Son Jesus Christ our Lord.

COLLECT

Reflection by **Guli Francis-Dehqani**

47

Morning Prayer – a simple form

Preparation

O Lord, open our lips
and our mouth shall proclaim your praise.

A prayer of thanksgiving for Lent *(for Passiontide see p. 50)*

Blessed are you, Lord God of our salvation,
to you be glory and praise for ever.
In the darkness of our sin you have shone in our hearts
to give the light of the knowledge of the glory of God
in the face of Jesus Christ.
Open our eyes to acknowledge your presence,
that freed from the misery of sin and shame
we may grow into your likeness from glory to glory.
Blessed be God, Father, Son and Holy Spirit.
Blessed be God for ever.

Word of God

Psalmody *(the psalm or psalms listed for the day)*

Glory to the Father and to the Son
and to the Holy Spirit;
as it was in the beginning is now:
and shall be for ever. Amen.

Reading from Holy Scripture *(one or both of the passages set for the day)*

Reflection

The Benedictus (The Song of Zechariah) *(see opposite page)*

Prayers

Intercessions – a time of prayer for the day and its tasks, the world and its need, the church and her life.

The Collect for the Day

The Lord's Prayer *(see p. 51)*

Conclusion

A blessing or the Grace *(see p. 51)*, or a concluding response

Let us bless the Lord
Thanks be to God

Benedictus (The Song of Zechariah)

1   Blessed be the Lord the God of Israel, ◆
    who has come to his people and set them free.

2   He has raised up for us a mighty Saviour, ◆
    born of the house of his servant David.

3   Through his holy prophets God promised of old ◆
    to save us from our enemies,
        from the hands of all that hate us,

4   To show mercy to our ancestors, ◆
    and to remember his holy covenant.

5   This was the oath God swore to our father Abraham: ◆
    to set us free from the hands of our enemies,

6   Free to worship him without fear, ◆
    holy and righteous in his sight
        all the days of our life.

7   And you, child, shall be called the prophet of the Most High, ◆
    for you will go before the Lord to prepare his way,

8   To give his people knowledge of salvation ◆
    by the forgiveness of all their sins.

9   In the tender compassion of our God ◆
    the dawn from on high shall break upon us,

10 To shine on those who dwell in darkness
        and the shadow of death, ◆
    and to guide our feet into the way of peace.

Luke 1.68-79

**Glory to the Father and to the Son
and to the Holy Spirit;
as it was in the beginning is now:
and shall be for ever. Amen.**

Seasonal Prayers of Thanksgiving

Passiontide

Blessed are you, Lord God of our salvation,
to you be praise and glory for ever.
As a man of sorrows and acquainted with grief
your only Son was lifted up
that he might draw the whole world to himself.
May we walk this day in the way of the cross
and always be ready to share its weight,
declaring your love for all the world.
Blessed be God, Father, Son and Holy Spirit.
Blessed be God for ever.

At Any Time

Blessed are you, creator of all,
to you be praise and glory for ever.
As your dawn renews the face of the earth
bringing light and life to all creation,
may we rejoice in this day you have made;
as we wake refreshed from the depths of sleep,
open our eyes to behold your presence
and strengthen our hands to do your will,
that the world may rejoice and give you praise.
Blessed be God, Father, Son and Holy Spirit.
Blessed be God for ever.

after Lancelot Andrewes (1626)

The Lord's Prayer and The Grace

Our Father in heaven,
hallowed be your name,
your kingdom come,
your will be done,
on earth as in heaven.
Give us today our daily bread.
Forgive us our sins
as we forgive those who sin against us.
Lead us not into temptation
but deliver us from evil.
For the kingdom, the power,
and the glory are yours
now and for ever.
Amen.

(or)

Our Father, who art in heaven,
hallowed be thy name;
thy kingdom come;
thy will be done;
on earth as it is in heaven.
Give us this day our daily bread.
And forgive us our trespasses,
as we forgive those who trespass against us.
And lead us not into temptation;
but deliver us from evil.
For thine is the kingdom,
the power and the glory,
for ever and ever.
Amen.

The grace of our Lord Jesus Christ,
and the love of God,
and the fellowship of the Holy Spirit,
be with us all evermore.
Amen.

An Order for Night Prayer (Compline)

The Lord almighty grant us a quiet night and a perfect end.
Amen.

Our help is in the name of the Lord
who made heaven and earth.

A period of silence for reflection on the past day may follow.

The following or other suitable words of penitence may be used

**Most merciful God,
we confess to you,
before the whole company of heaven and one another,
that we have sinned in thought, word and deed
and in what we have failed to do.
Forgive us our sins,
heal us by your Spirit
and raise us to new life in Christ. Amen.**

O God, make speed to save us.
O Lord, make haste to help us.

**Glory to the Father and to the Son
and to the Holy Spirit;
as it was in the beginning is now
and shall be for ever. Amen.
Alleluia.**

The following or another suitable hymn may be sung

Before the ending of the day,
Creator of the world, we pray
That you, with steadfast love, would keep
Your watch around us while we sleep.

From evil dreams defend our sight,
From fears and terrors of the night;
Tread underfoot our deadly foe
That we no sinful thought may know.

O Father, that we ask be done
Through Jesus Christ, your only Son;
And Holy Spirit, by whose breath
Our souls are raised to life from death.

The Word of God

One or more of Psalms 4, 91 or 134 may be used.

Psalm 134

1   Come, bless the Lord, all you servants of the Lord, ♦
    you that by night stand in the house of the Lord.

2   Lift up your hands towards the sanctuary ♦
    and bless the Lord.

3   The Lord who made heaven and earth ♦
    give you blessing out of Zion.

**Glory to the Father and to the Son
and to the Holy Spirit;
as it was in the beginning is now
and shall be for ever. Amen.**

Scripture Reading

*One of the following short lessons or another suitable
passage is read*

You, O Lord, are in the midst of us and we are called by your
name; leave us not, O Lord our God.

Jeremiah 14.9

(or)

Be sober, be vigilant, because your adversary the devil is
prowling round like a roaring lion, seeking for someone
to devour. Resist him, strong in the faith.

1 Peter 5.8,9

(or)

The servants of the Lamb shall see the face of God, whose name
will be on their foreheads. There will be no more night: they will
not need the light of a lamp or the light of the sun, for God will
be their light, and they will reign for ever and ever.

Revelation 22.4,5

The following responsory may be said

Into your hands, O Lord, I commend my spirit.
Into your hands, O Lord, I commend my spirit.
For you have redeemed me, Lord God of truth.
I commend my spirit.
Glory to the Father and to the Son
and to the Holy Spirit.
Into your hands, O Lord, I commend my spirit.

Or, in Easter

Into your hands, O Lord, I commend my spirit.
    Alleluia, alleluia.
Into your hands, O Lord, I commend my spirit.
    Alleluia, alleluia.
For you have redeemed me, Lord God of truth.
Alleluia, alleluia.
Glory to the Father and to the Son
and to the Holy Spirit.
Into your hands, O Lord, I commend my spirit.
    Alleluia, alleluia.

Keep me as the apple of your eye.
Hide me under the shadow of your wings.

Gospel Canticle

Nunc Dimittis (The Song of Simeon)

Save us, O Lord, while waking,
and guard us while sleeping,
that awake we may watch with Christ
and asleep may rest in peace.

1   Now, Lord, you let your servant go in peace:
      your word has been fulfilled.

2   My own eyes have seen the salvation
      which you have prepared in the sight of every people;

3   A light to reveal you to the nations
      and the glory of your people Israel.

Luke 2.29-32

Glory to the Father and to the Son
and to the Holy Spirit;
as it was in the beginning is now
and shall be for ever. Amen.

Save us, O Lord, while waking,
and guard us while sleeping,
that awake we may watch with Christ
and asleep may rest in peace.

Prayers

Intercessions and thanksgivings may be offered here.

The Collect

Visit this place, O Lord, we pray,
and drive far from it the snares of the enemy;
may your holy angels dwell with us and guard us in peace,
and may your blessing be always upon us;
through Jesus Christ our Lord.
Amen.

The Lord's Prayer (see p. 51) may be said.

The Conclusion

In peace we will lie down and sleep;
for you alone, Lord, make us dwell in safety.

Abide with us, Lord Jesus,
for the night is at hand and the day is now past.

As the night watch looks for the morning,
so do we look for you, O Christ.

[Come with the dawning of the day
and make yourself known in the breaking of the bread.]

The Lord bless us and watch over us;
the Lord make his face shine upon us and be gracious to us;
the Lord look kindly on us and give us peace.
Amen.

Love what you've read?

Why not consider using
Reflections for Daily Prayer
all year round? We also
publish these meditations
on Bible readings in an
annual format, containing
material for the entire
Church year.

The volume for 2021/22
will be published in
May 2021 and features
contributions from a host
of distinguished writers:
Justine Allain Chapman,
Joanna Collicutt, Stephen Cottrell,
Azariah France-Williams, Guli Francis-Dehqani,
Malcolm Guite, Isabelle Hamley, Colin Heber-Percy,
Christopher Herbert, David Hoyle, John Inge, Rachel
Mann, Anna Matthews, Peter Moger, Philip North,
Karen O'Donnell, Brother Sam SSF, Angela Tilby,
Rachel Treweek, Catherine Williams, Rowan Williams.

Reflections for Daily Prayer:
Advent 2021 to the eve of Advent 2022

ISBN 978 0 7151 2383 6
£16.99 • Available May 2021

REFLECTIONS FOR DAILY PRAYER
App

Make Bible study and reflection a part of your routine wherever you go with the Reflections for Daily Prayer App for Apple and Android devices.

Download the app for free from the App Store (Apple devices) or Google Play (Android devices) and receive a week's worth of reflections free. Then purchase a monthly, three-monthly or annual subscription to receive up-to-date content.

REFLECTIONS FOR SUNDAYS (YEAR B)

Reflections for Sundays offers over 250 reflections on the Principal Readings for every Sunday and major Holy Day in Year B, from the same experienced team of writers that have made *Reflections for Daily Prayer* so successful. For each Sunday and major Holy Day, they provide:

- full lectionary details for the Principal Service
- a reflection on each Old Testament reading (both Continuous and Related)
- a reflection on the Epistle
- a reflection on the Gospel.

This book also contains a substantial introduction to the Gospels of Mark and Luke, written by Paula Gooder.

£14.99 • 288 pages
ISBN 978 1 78140 030 2

Also available in Kindle and epub formats

REFLECTIONS ON THE PSALMS

£14.99 • 192 pages
ISBN 978 0 7151 4490 9

Reflections on the Psalms provides original and insightful meditations on each of the Bible's 150 Psalms.

Each reflection is accompanied by its corresponding Psalm refrain and prayer from the *Common Worship Psalter*, making this a valuable resource for personal or devotional use.

Specially written introductions by Paula Gooder and Steven Croft explore the Psalms and the Bible and the Psalms in the life of the Church.